TURN YOUR HOLIDAYS INTO HOLY-DAYS

31 Day Guide to a Happy Healthy December

Marsha Apsley

1

Marsha Apsley
Visit my website at www.marshaapsley.com

Printed in the United States of America

First Printing: October 2018

ISBN-13: 9781726075893

To my guys. Kent, Ben, and Ethan are God's greatest gifts to me.

Thank you to Markita, Carol, Brandi, Dyan, Earlene, and Angela for meticulously reading through the book in advance and giving me valuable feedback. And thank you to all the gals in the Faith and Fitness Sisterhood for helping me with the title of the book and for being the most amazing community of women.

CONTENTS

PREFACE

Christmas is my favorite time of year.

I love Christmas music and Christmas lights and Christmas cookies.

I love giving and receiving gifts. I love the decorations. And a cup of hot coffee or hot chocolate tastes better at Christmastime.

I love running in the chill of the early morning hours and seeing twinkling lights and festive decorations.

I love the reason why we celebrate.

I love reading the Christmas story in the Bible, because it's not simply a story. It's history. It's real life. A baby was born in a manger. Our Savior came to the world as a human and rested in the arms of a young girl who could not comprehend what this all meant, but she knew something was different about her Son.

Christmastime is a special time. There is no season quite like it. It's a time when all the world pauses to acknowledge a holy happening.

But still, we can get caught up in all of the fun and festivities. We can get distracted with shopping lists and party invites. We find ourselves rushing from one activity to the next trying to fit it all in and enjoy every last ounce of the joyous season.

This wasn't how the very first Christmas happened.

It was quiet.

There weren't lights and decorations and dinners. There was no Santa with his reindeer and bag full of toys.

There were a few small gifts, glorious music, and a young family doing the best they knew how.

While Christmas indeed is a time to celebrate and gather together, a time to give and receive gifts and to sing and make merry, let us make time to get quiet.

May we quiet our hearts and our homes.

May we still our minds and slow our schedules.

Let this be a Christmas season that will last in our hearts all year long.

INTRODUCTION

This book is designed to help you make the most of your Christmas holiday.

Each day you'll find an entry. It may be a healthy living tip, a fun activity, or a short devotional.

The first part of the book gives you daily tips and activities to find the balance needed to enjoy this time of year.

As we get closer to Christmas, you'll notice that the focus is on God's Word and setting our hearts and minds squarely on the reason we celebrate this season.

The final entries will help you gear up for the year ahead without forgetting about the significance of what we have just celebrated.

My prayer for you is that you will have a blessed month and take the peace and joy of the holiday season into your new year.

DECEMBER 1

Christmas Anticipation

If you're a runner in Indiana, and if friends and family know you're a runner in Indiana, what question do you start hearing as the month of May gets closer? "Are you running *The Mini*?" Here in Indiana everybody knows what *The Mini* is. It's only the largest half marathon around. It's the 500 Festival Mini Marathon. You know, that 13.1 mile race that's run on the first Saturday of May that takes you around the Indianapolis Motor Speedway? I've run that race 20 times. I've run both my fastest and my slowest half marathon times at this event.

Training plans for this race usually begin in February, and weekly long runs get back on the calendar if you've taken a little break. *Everybody* knows it's that time of year. In April you have your last long run followed by your taper. Even though the big day is looming, you must slow down and reduce mileage. Any good training plan includes this very important piece, the taper, the slow down. You must have this so you'll be ready for the big day, so your mind and body will be prepared.

The month of December and the Christmas season come with much of the same excitement and anticipation as does preparing for *The Mini*. Children start making their lists. Parties are planned. Shopping commences. So much to do. So much to take in.

Excitement fills the air. There is the Christmas countdown. The advent calendars. Cooking. Baking. Present wrapping. Black Friday. Cyber Monday. Everything is big and bright. There are jingles and bells. The list could go on and on.

This is a fun time. It's a joyous time. A hope-filled time. It's a time filled with laughter and good cheer. But the time is *filled*. It's *full*.

Our racing preparation is full as well with intervals, long runs, cross training, hill repeats, and stretching. But we also need to keep our focus and not get caught up with all the expectations and everyone else's goals. In much the same way, we must take time to focus our attention inward this month to what matters most in our homes during the Christmas season.

How can we do that? It's all about tapering. It's about slowing down and making time to quiet our hearts. For a marathon taper, athletes are advised to stick to a good sleep schedule. They are told to continue to fill their bodies with proper nutrition while filling their minds with positive thoughts and encouraging words.

Let's do that over the next few weeks prior to our big day...to Christmas!

- Get enough rest.
- Fill your body with proper nutrition.
- Spend time with the ones you love.
- Fill your mind with the Word.

*"When they saw the star, they rejoiced exceedingly with great joy."
Matthew 2:10 (NKJV)*

*"And the angel said to them, 'Fear not, for behold, I bring you good
news of great joy that will be for all the people." Luke 2:10 (KJV)*

*"And the Word was made flesh, and dwelt among us, (and we beheld
his glory, the glory as of the only begotten of the Father,) full of grace
and truth." John 1:14 (KJV)*

*"For unto us a child is born, unto us a son is given: and the
government shall be upon his shoulder: and his name shall be called
Wonderful, Counsellor, The mighty God, The everlasting Father, The
Prince of Peace." Isaiah 9:6 (KJV)*

May your December be filled with anticipation as well as times of calm
and quiet reflection.

DECEMBER 2

Granny O's Fudge

Part of the fun of Christmas is all the goodies.

Tip: Enjoy dishes and treats that you normally don't get the chance to have all year long.

Chips and various dips? Those show up everywhere throughout the year. Maybe skip the appetizers and go for a small helping of Aunt Carol's dressing or Aunt Lynn's noodles that you only get once or twice a year.

And what about all the desserts? Chocolate chip cookies and cupcakes happen all the time. But something like my Granny O's fudge only happened about once a year.

My Granny O has been gone several years now, but I still get requests for her peanut butter fudge. I have no idea where she got this recipe. It may have been on a product label at one time; I only have it written in a recipe book that I've had for years.

Part of a healthy holiday includes enjoying sweet memories and sweet treats. I'm going to start with a batch of Granny O's fudge.

Granny O's Peanut Butter Fudge

¾ cup butter

3 cups sugar

⅔ cup evaporated milk (can use skim)

1 package peanut butter chips (+ about ⅓ of another package for good measure!)

1 jar Marshmallow Crème (7oz)

1 tsp. vanilla

Lightly grease 13X9 pan (or line with parchment paper). For thick slices, use 8X8 or 9X9.

Microwave butter in a 2-quart bowl on high for 1 minute, or until melted (be sure to cover loosely with paper towel or lid). Add sugar and milk. Mix well. Microwave 3 minutes, stir. Microwave 2 more minutes, stir. (This should get it to a boil). Microwave another 3 minutes, stir. (Watch it during this time. It has boiled over on me before. I think the butter makes it boil more quickly than margarine.) Microwave 2-1/2 more minutes. (If it started boiling a lot during the previous 3 minutes and you had to stop it before that time was up, you might not need to microwave a full 2-1/2 minutes…this is the touchy part!) Remove from the microwave and gradually stir in chips until melted. Add marshmallow crème and vanilla. Mix well. Pour into prepared pan. Cool completely at room temp. Cut into squares.

Optional: stir in pecans. You can also use chocolate chips instead of the peanut butter chips to make chocolate fudge.

Note: Fudge can be stored in freezer then taken out and ready to eat anytime to satisfy a sweet tooth.

DECEMBER 3

Tips to Thrive

There often seems to be two approaches to the month of December: just survive or savor every moment. I hope that you are ready to savor every moment and not let the month and all the activities overwhelm you.

Here are a few things that will help you not only *survive* the holidays, but *thrive*, during this holiday season. Pick one or more to incorporate each day or throughout the month.

1. Daily quiet time. Whether you choose a short passage of scripture, a Bible study, or soft music and prayer time, taking a few minutes to get quiet and be with the Lord will make all the difference in how this month goes. If our hearts are not prepared, nothing else is likely to fall into place.

2. Breakfast. It's key to a good day. I go through phases with breakfast. Sometimes it's a shake. Other times I eat oatmeal everyday for three weeks. If my workout comes later in the day, I may have a protein bar. Lately I've fixed a piece or two of whole grain toast with a little nut butter, honey, and cinnamon.

3. Get enough sleep. Keep to your schedule. Whatever your sleep schedule, try to keep to it and get seven to eight hours of sleep.

4. Stay hydrated...with water! If you're having a cocktail then drink extra water. Be careful not to drink your calories.

5. Move. Register for a 5K. I love the Santa Hustle series that happens every year in Indianapolis. I imagine wherever you are there is a holiday run. Don't work out to punish yourself or exercise out of guilt. Do it to stick with your schedule. Make fresh air a daily priority.

6. Manage stress with things like yoga, a leisure walk, hot bath, hot tea, a book, or Christmas music.

7. Focus on protein. Make lean protein the focus at each meal and snack. Protein fills you up and gives you energy.

8. Accountability. Keep up with your running or walking partner. Use an app. Keep a workout journal.

9. Be prepared. Pack a bar or small snack so you always have something with you that's a healthy option if you get caught in traffic, shop a little longer than anticipated, visit with a friend, etc.

10. Most of all, ENJOY this time of year!

DECEMBER 4

Morning Routine

Let's face it. Not everyone is a morning person. But the morning comes everyday and most of our responsibilities, be it a job, school, parenting, etc., require us to get up and get going in the mornings.

The holiday season includes extra activities and a few late nights, but that doesn't mean that our daily responsibilities go away. It will be important for us to keep to our morning routine so that we can approach each day with intention and get everything done that needs to be accomplished.

Although I would classify myself as a morning person, mornings still don't come super easy for me. Many days I'd much rather hit the snooze button and skip the entire morning. But I've been doing this enough that I know as soon as my feet hit the floor, things start looking up.

I'm not going to try to convert you into a morning person, but I can help you develop a morning routine that will get your day started a little better than it might be right now.

For starters, a good morning begins the night before. In fact, much of my preparation for a good day starts the prior evening.

Things to do the evening before to help you have a better morning

1. Plan - *Meals, Clothes, Workout*

If your coffee pot has a timer, have it set and ready to go. Even if there is no timer, you can have the coffee in the basket and be ready to pour in water and turn it on.

What will you eat for breakfast? Perhaps you can prepare overnight oats. You might want to have some healthy bars available to take on the road.

Workout clothes and work clothes. Have them laid out the night before. This serves two purposes. One, no excuse for skipping the morning workout. Clothes are ready. If you are working out midday or after work, have your bag packed. And when you have your work day clothes laid out, you save yourself time deciding what to wear.

Know your workout plan for the day, or even the week. Every weekend, I plan my workouts and write them on the calendar. That way I don't have to decide what workout I'll do each morning. Look at the weather to determine which workouts will take place outside and which days you might need to plan an indoor workout. If you can, register for a class ahead of time. This will help with accountability.

2. Wind down

Start unplugging and winding down at least 30 minutes prior to bedtime if you can. Let's face it, there are more parties and activities to attend right now so evening time might be busier than usual. Still, it's important to give yourself time to wind down, maybe with a cup of hot tea and a book or visiting with your family and watching something fun on television.

3. Sleep

There's nothing that can take the place of a good night's rest.

As you can see, our evenings are very important to a good morning.

Now that we have things planned and prepared for the morning and hopefully have gotten a good night's rest, when the alarm goes off, we increase our chance at getting up and going.

But if getting out of bed is still a bit difficult, try these things:

Set your alarm to allow you to hit snooze one time. This way you don't have to jump right out of bed.

If hitting snooze way too many times is an issue, put your alarm across the room so that you have to get out of bed to turn it off.

When I hear my alarm, the thought crosses my mind to shut it off and roll over and go back to sleep...for the entire day!

Instead I recite Psalm 118:24 *"This is the day the Lord has made, I will rejoice and be glad in it."* You may want to put this on a Post It note on your alarm or frame it by your bed. This helps motivate me to get up with an expectation that God has a plan for me for the day. Perhaps you prefer another scripture or quote that you find motivating. The key is to grab onto some motivation to get those feet on the floor.

Once you're up, you can get your workout clothes that are already laid out and hit the bathroom to wash your face and brush your teeth. (Use cold water! There's nothing like a splash of cold water to wake you up!)

Next comes ice water and some stretches.

My first drink is ice water and then I lay down in the middle of the floor and stretch just to loosen my body.

While I do my quiet time, I drink warm water with a splash of lemon. Lemon is said to have some detoxifying effects on your body. I like the flavor, and I have found that it's good practice to get a head start on my water consumption before going for the coffee.

Quiet time and workout are two keys that make or break my day.

This bit of time in the morning doesn't have to be long and can be adjusted to your preferences. The key is to give yourself a little time to get your mind and body focused for the day.

By now you should be ready to hit the shower and get on with the rest of your day.

Final note… *Give yourself some time.*

You may want to start by setting your alarm five minutes earlier or drinking a glass of water before the first cup of coffee. Perhaps you'll start the evening before with some of those preparations.

If mornings are difficult for you, do this in pieces. Try one change a week until you get there.

DECEMBER 5

Dealing with Sweets

The holiday season isn't anything if it isn't the food season. Sweets and treats and dinners everywhere you turn.

If we don't handle this time well, we'll be making New Year's resolutions driven by guilt and remorse brought on from eating too much sugar and junk over the holidays.

But it doesn't have to be that way. We can navigate these times, not by avoiding them, but by enjoying them and wake up January 1 with the same plan as we had on October 31st and December 25th.

Incorporate the following tips to make healthier choices at the dessert table and when you're preparing your favorite sweet treats.

1. **Chocolate** – Choose dark chocolate. It's known to contain antioxidants, has less sugar, and most of the time dairy free.

2. **Nuts** - Nuts add some protein and healthy fat and therefore give you a sense of fullness - a feeling that doesn't often result

from a sugary carb. For instance, choose almond or peanut chocolate candies rather than plain.

3. **Flour options** when baking - Oat flour, almond meal, and coconut flour are all good choices if you choose to bake a treat for your family or visitors. For the most part, these flours can be substituted 1:1 for regular flour.

4. **Sweeteners** - Natural sweeteners like honey, pure maple syrup, and stevia are some options to consider. Coconut sugar is another popular option. Stay away from high fructose corn syrup and artificial sweeteners. In some recipes reducing the amount of sugar called for doesn't have much impact on the outcome. Do you have a cookie recipe that calls for one cup of sugar? Simply reduce by one-fourth to one-half. No one will notice!

5. **Protein powder** - This is another option to add a little flavor (vanilla or chocolate) in the place of the sugar and/or flour. You might have to play around with it.

6. **Water** - I can't emphasize enough the importance of drinking water. If you do nothing else over the course of the holiday season, drink water. Aim for half your body weight in ounces each day. This will automatically reduce your desire to be drinking other things like cocktails, sugary sodas, or hot drinks with all the extras. Consider warm water with lemon to start your day and a cup of decaf green tea to finish off your day.

7. **Move** – Aim to include movement into each day. You don't have to spend an hour at the gym. It can simply be a walk around the block after dinner. Take 15 minutes to stretch to start or end your day. Pick up a pair of dumbbells and do some bicep curls, tricep kickbacks, and squats. Keep it simple; just move.

To be clear, sugar is not the enemy. But, it can be troublesome. We know that our bodies don't work efficiently on sugary foods. Sugar does not sustain our energy. It doesn't build muscle. However, in moderation, sweets and treats are okay and enjoyable.

The point of this time of year, and really every day, is to live it and enjoy it to the fullest.

DECEMBER 6

St. Nicholas Day and other traditions

Today is St. Nicholas Day. Some people observe this holiday by setting out shoes and then leaving treats in them for the children.

Advent Calendar. How fun is it to have the Christmas countdown? We always have at least one (and it often includes chocolate!).

Birthday cake for Jesus. When Ethan was younger, we had a Happy Birthday Jesus party with his friends. We enjoyed cake and crafts and games. Instead of exchanging gifts, everyone brought non-perishable food items, and we donated them to a local food pantry.

What about an evening drive with hot chocolate to look at Christmas lights?

The point of today is to encourage you to have a tradition, or possibly multiple traditions, to make this time memorable for you and your loved ones.

Plan a fun activity. Plan a few fun activities to determine which ones your family really enjoys. What sticks with them?

You may also consider a tradition all your own.

One of mine is my early morning Christmas Day run. I get up as early as I have to (thankfully my family has never been super early risers on Christmas morning), and I go out for a run through the quiet streets. I take in all the lights and notice houses that are still quiet and the ones that appear awake and celebrating.

My husband stays up late and wraps Christmas presents for our family during Sunday night or Monday night football (usually the last one before Christmas Day!).

Come up with something fun to do this month with your family as well as something special just for you.

DECEMBER 7

Winter Workout Tips

Christmastime and winter in Shelbyville, Indiana usually means snow, ice, and cold weather at some point. But these weather conditions don't have to cancel our plans for living an active lifestyle.

These tips will keep you safe and warm and full of a sunny spirit.

1. **Attitude** - In all things, we must be grateful. See the beauty of the snow. Take the opportunity to sip more slowly on a hot drink on an especially cold day. Watch with amazement as the fluffy flakes fall to the ground.

2. **The right gear** - Layers! You can find fabrics that are windproof, waterproof, and weatherproof. They will come in handy in extreme conditions. Layer up. Wear a base layer that will wick away the sweat and then layer over with something that is preferably windproof and waterproof.

3. **Cover all the extremities** - Hands, feet, ears, head. You may need two pair of gloves and socks if you don't have any heavy-duty wool. You may need a face mask. There are some special ones that will cover your mouth and nose but still have tiny holes so you can breathe! (That's important!)

4. **Drink hot stuff** - I love my coffee every morning, but on cold wintry days it becomes even more essential. And what about an evening cup of hot tea? Before you go out, warm up with something hot and have something hot when you come in. This will get right to your core and get you warming up quickly.

5. **Enjoy a hot shower or bath** - This may warm your body, but it can also be relaxing and put your mind at ease if you've been tensed up driving on icy roads or dealing with a busy schedule.

6. **Moisturize** - I don't know about you, but my skin gets so dry in the winter. My hands are cracking. My skin is itchy. I love Bass Farms (local Shelbyville, Indiana business) lotions and especially their Triple B moisturizing cream for extremely dry skin. Find a good moisturizer and use it daily.

7. **Be flexible with your exercise plan** - There's a reason the racing season doesn't ramp up until April or May. January and February can be hard to get in those long runs. There will be time to increase your mileage. The key is to stay consistent.

8. **Split your workouts** - If 6 miles was on your schedule, but it's way too cold or the snow and ice are making it difficult, do three miles inside and three outside.

9. **Work out inside** - Hit the weights. Ride your trainer. Use a treadmill. Tip: Use time on the treadmill or trainer for intervals. It'll keep you focused, adds variety, and helps the time pass more quickly.

10. **Play** - If you have snow, go play in it!!! Be a kid! I see snow in the forecast, and my reaction is "ugh." My son sees snow in the forecast, and he's whooping and hollering! This brings us back to the first tip...our attitude!

DECEMBER 8

Stay Organized

How do you stay organized? How do you manage your time so that you can work, take care of the house and the little ones, and still have time to work out and take care of your body?

These questions come all year long, but during the holidays time management and staying organized is even tougher - yet it's the most desired outcome.

I'll admit that being organized, managing my time, and sticking to a routine comes somewhat naturally. I do better overall in this scenario. It's my default mode. But I will add this disclaimer: our greatest strengths can become our greatest weaknesses. I know that I can tend towards being too rigid at times, so I have to work on letting go a little, especially during this season. Nevertheless, things do go more smoothly when we have some sense of organization and time management.

A few tips on how to stay organized by essentially simplifying and spreading out tasks:

Around the house

- Clean a little everyday.

    - After you brush your teeth, wipe down the sink.

    - Every few days, clean the mirror in the bathroom.

    - Keep sanitizing wipes in the bathrooms and under the kitchen sink so you can wipe things off quickly

    - Dust off furniture in the main living areas regularly.

- Do a load of laundry each day.

- Keep things picked up and put in place by having a spot for things (and letting family members know where that is).

Fitness

- Lay clothes out the night before.

- Write out your plan for the week. List what workouts you plan to do and when you plan to do them.

- Get some accountability.

- Let go of the notion that you must have a gym membership or an hour a day to make it count. This thought alone paralyzes people into doing nothing.

- Make games or a walk after dinner part of your holiday celebrations. Don't be afraid to bundle up and get outside for some fresh air.

Meal Planning

- I don't advocate living out of plastic containers, but it's helpful to have a general idea of what you're going to eat for the coming week and what you'll fix for meals.

- Consider everyone's schedule then get things out of the freezer and into the refrigerator a couple of days prior to when you'll fix it.

- Utilize grocery store pick up.

Schedule

- Keep to a regular sleep schedule.

- Have a calendar so that everyone is aware what's going on. Preview the week's activities.

Get others to help

- Make a chore list.

- Assign designated places for shoes, coats, backpacks, etc.

Make a list

- List the top three things you must accomplish each day for home, family, and work.

- List projects that you're working on. Spend a little time on those when time allows. Add a deadline.

Bonus Tip: Each season set aside some time to get organized. For instance, at the beginning of summer break, take the first few days to clean up and organize. The end of the school year gets quite busy. Take time to regroup and refocus on your organizational skills.

The same goes with the holiday season. There will be a few things that get missed and put aside until January. The daily schedule will get interrupted, and we might miss some sleep here and there. Not every workout will get checked off. Yet, the key is to have a plan and stick with it as much as possible.

We're not meant to live life in a state of overwhelm.

Philippians 4:6-7 (NIV) says, *"Do not be anxious about anything, but in every situation, by prayer and petition, with thanksgiving, present your requests to God. And the peace of God, which transcends all understanding, will guard your hearts and your minds in Christ Jesus."*

Pick a tip or two from the list that will work for your situation. Simplifying or streamlining one or two things can help relieve some of your stress and overwhelm and help you get organized so you can fully enjoy the holiday season.

DECEMBER 9

Self-care

Self-care is not selfish. Not even during the season of giving. In fact, it may be more important during this time of year. Why? If we're not at our best, physically, emotionally, spiritually, then we won't be good for other people. At this special time of year, we want to be truly present with the people that we love and make memories together.

If you need a time out, it's okay. In fact, it's important to make time for yourself. It may be as simple as fifteen minutes alone by the fireplace sipping on hot tea in the evening. Or you may want to schedule a massage or a manicure this month.

If we rush through this month and get caught up in all the hustle and bustle, come January we'll regret the lost time.

Some ideas

Fix a cup of hot chocolate and add a candy cane.

Take a drive, turn on Christmas music, and look at the lights.

Color.

Read a Christmas novel.

Bake cookies.

Schedule coffee with a friend.

Sit by the fireplace.

Get your hair done.

Stop at church and sit in the Lord's presence.

The list could go on and on. The important thing is that you don't lose *you* in the middle of this month.

DECEMBER 10

Ways to Healthify Your Menu

Do you feel like a healthy diet must consist of salad and grilled chicken everyday?

My son asked me one evening "What's for dinner?" My husband sarcastically replied, "Chicken, chicken, or chicken?"

I'll admit I could get by with eating the same thing everyday. (Remember routine?) I don't mind that my daily meals are pretty much the same, but my family wants a little variety.

So how do you keep some variety and stick with healthy choices? Especially during the holiday season?

First tip: Do your best. Maintain your healthy eating habits as well as you can. Then when the parties come around, you'll feel better about trying some bites of a variety of foods.

Consider the following ways to healthify your daily food choices.

Protein and Dairy Options

In addition to chicken, consider adding turkey, pork, venison, and lean cuts of beef to the menu. Pick up ready-to-go packets of tuna.

Low fat cottage cheese is a good source of protein as well as nonfat plain Greek yogurt. In recipes calling for cream cheese, try low fat or nonfat cream cheese or Greek yogurt.

In recipes calling for sour cream, substitute with plain Greek yogurt.

When it comes to milk, consider gradually switching from whole to 2% to 1% to maybe even skim. There are several dairy-free alternatives as well. Use unsweetened almond milk in some recipes. This offers a reduction in calories, and the lactose in regular milk has a negative effect on some tummies.

Salad Menu

You can do so much with a salad. After the lettuce, toss in all kinds of cut up vegetables, maybe even some fresh fruit (grapes, strawberries, or oranges), dried fruit (raisins, tart cherries), low fat cheese, lean protein, a few nuts (slivered almonds or walnuts).

Dessert Menu

Oat flour is great for baking. Other options include almond flour, coconut flour, and whole wheat flour. (Be sure to read about measuring, leavening, and liquid adjustments if you use a different type of flour.) For sweeteners consider using stevia. Honey and pure maple syrup can be used in some recipes. Coconut oil is very popular these days in both solid or liquid form to replace oils or butter in a recipe. Protein powder is also an option to add a little flavor (vanilla or chocolate) in the place of the sugar and/or flour.

These are just a few quick ideas to get you thinking about how to make small changes to recipes to either add nutrition or lessen the fat, calories, and processed ingredients.

Get creative! Don't be afraid to try some new tricks when you're in the kitchen! Try one out for your next pitch in. It might become a crowd favorite.

DECEMBER 11

Benefits of the Kitchen Freezer

The kitchen is one of the most popular and most used rooms of a home. It can make us or break us some days. But we do have to eat, right?! During the holidays we spend a lot of time in the kitchen preparing food and gathering there with friends and family. Let's use it wisely and make the most of it.

One of the most valuable tools in the kitchen for healthy living is the freezer.

Ice

Drinking water is so important to a healthy body. For chilled water, add ice. Ice in your morning shake makes it much thicker and gives it more volume which adds to your feeling of fullness.

Frozen Food

Frozen berries are good for snacks or to add to a shake. Especially during this time of year, it's hard to find good fresh fruit. Use frozen, preferably the no sugar added variety. Stock up on lean meats. Ice cream anyone? In my opinion, it's never too cold for ice cream. There are healthy options. Some are dairy free. Some have protein in them. Take a little time to read labels the next time you're in the ice cream aisle at the grocery store. One trick is to put a container of plain Greek yogurt in the freezer while you're eating dinner. When you're finished, it's frozen just enough to taste like ice cream (add a tablespoon of chocolate chips, and it's perfect!).

Hiding Place

Yes, the freezer is a great hiding place for foods you want readily available, but you don't want them to be at your fingertips. How about your dark chocolate? There's nothing wrong with a chocolate here and there, but if it's in plain sight, it's easier to grab without even thinking.

Storage

You can make ahead most anything and freeze it until you're ready to use it. I make a big batch of protein balls* and store them in the freezer for a handy snack. Remember that fudge recipe I shared? It stores well in the freezer. Instead of spreading out holiday baking over several days or making a new batch of fudge or cookies every time you need one, get all the baking done in one day and then freeze it all. You'll have what you need when the occasion calls for it.

*My simple protein ball recipe: Mix together 1 cup nut butter of choice, ½ cup honey or pure maple syrup, 1 cup protein powder, 1 cup oats, a few mini chocolate chips. Shape into balls and freeze.

How will you use your freezer this month?

DECEMBER 12

Christmas Memories and Check In

Grandpa and Granny O coming to our house on Christmas morning to see what Santa brought.

The year all the gifts were from Santa, and none were from Mom and Dad.

Driving around and looking at Christmas lights.

Baking a birthday cake for Jesus.

Being a newlywed and sleeping in the living room with the Christmas tree.

Ben sleeping until Noon on Christmas Day.

Ethan determined to see Santa's bag.

The last Christmas with Papaw Bob.

These are just a few sweet memories that come to mind when I think of Christmas over the years.

Christmastime is for making memories. It's a time for us to slow down and enjoy the season. It's time for us to celebrate the birth of our Savior. The best present we can give is our time and to be present for those with whom we come into contact...our family, our friends, and the stranger at the shopping center.

Tomorrow this book takes a bit of a turn as we prime our hearts more towards our Savior and the reason for this season. Each of the next twelve days we'll read a daily devotional to help us focus our hearts and our minds on Jesus.

Take a moment. Close your eyes. Breathe in and out. What do you smell? How does the air around you feel? What sounds do you hear? What memories of Christmases past flood in?

How are you doing so far this month? Are you feeling overwhelmed and exhausted? Have you enjoyed every minute of this month?

There is no right or wrong answer. Simply acknowledge where you are at this point. Choose how you want to move through the remainder of the month. Ask God to open your heart to His Word and to His presence in the coming days.

DECEMBER 13

"Be still, and know that I am God: I will be exalted among the heathen, I will be exalted in the earth." Psalm 46:10 (KJV)

The hustle and bustle of Christmas is fully upon us.

There are trees and twinkling lights. There's shopping to do and Christmas music playing in the background.

Perhaps the temperature is getting colder and it might be snowing where you are.

I absolutely love this time of the year!

But if I'm not careful, I will zip through it checking off tasks from my list and filling my calendar with as many activities as possible.

Are you the same?

Yes, many of those activities are good ones. There are gatherings with friends and family. School parties and plays. And, of course a Christmas 5K to run.

Yet in the midst of all of this, I hear *"Be still and know..."*

To fully experience this special time of year, we must first be still. We must take time to truly know the One we celebrate. He's the reason we have this season.

Be still and know.

As we enter the final weeks of this holiday season, let us choose to take time – daily – to be still and communicate with the One who makes this possible.

May we sip our coffee a bit slower. Perhaps we could linger by the fire a little longer. Take a few more minutes with our Savior.

Be still and know.

Prayer: Dear God, please quiet my heart and my mind. Help me to slow down so that I can experience the fullness of Your presence. In Jesus' name, Amen.

Activity: Take time out today. Close your eyes and sit in silence for five minutes. Practice pausing in His presence.

DECEMBER 14

"And the Word was made flesh, and dwelt among us, (and we beheld his glory, the glory as of the only begotten of the Father,) full of grace and truth." John 1:14 (KJV)

I don't think we can ever fully grasp what this means.

At Christmastime we celebrate that the God of the universe, the One who was and always has been, came down from Heaven to dwell among us - among you and me.

He came for *us*.

He took on flesh so that He could feel pain and hunger and sadness.

He counted it joy to face the cross for our salvation - for my salvation and yours.

If you were the only one, He would have done this. He loves you so much.

As we get closer to Christmas Day may we open our hearts to Who He is and to what He has done for us so that we can fully appreciate the meaning of the season.

Prayer: Dear Jesus, thank You for choosing me over the comfort of Heaven. Open my eyes to see where I can help others in need. In Your name I pray, Amen.

Activity: Jesus gave up the comfort of His heavenly home to come to Earth to dwell among us. What can you do today for someone in need? Consider dropping off a donation at a local food pantry or homeless shelter.

.

DECEMBER 15

"We love him, because he first loved us." 1 John 4:19 (KJV)

Love. Before we ever loved Him, *He* loved us.

Before my husband and I started dating, I remember someone telling me that a certain man was interested in me. At first they didn't tell me who, and honestly I had no idea who it could be. It took a long time for me to realize that it was the man who eventually became my husband.

I came to find out, he had his eye on me long before I acknowledged him.

Jesus loves you.

He's had His eye on you since before you were born. He knows you. And He loves you just as you are. He's watching from afar hoping that, if you haven't already, you will accept His love for you.

What a wonderful time of year to ponder the love of Christ for us!

Prayer: Thank you Jesus for Your ongoing and everlasting love. I open my heart and fully accept Your love for me. Help me to love others well. It's in Your name that I pray, Amen.

Activity: The greatest way to love Jesus is to share His love with others. Look for a chance to tell someone today that Jesus loves them.

DECEMBER 16

"See what great love the Father has lavished on us, that we should be called children of God! And that is what we are! The reason the world does not know us is that it did not know him. Dear friends, now we are children of God, and what we will be has not yet been made known. But we know that when Christ appears, we shall be like him, for we shall see him as he is. All who have this hope in him purify themselves, just as he is pure."
1 John 3:1-3 (NIV)

Hope.

Hope has come.

Jesus is the hope that this world needs. He came to Earth to be the hope for a world that didn't have any. It was a world that was tied to laws and sacrifices.

But He came so that we could become children of God and have a hope for our future.

Hope grows into confidence. The confidence of knowing that our future is secure in Christ.

Even though He was a tiny baby, they knew He was different. They may not have grasped exactly what it was, but the shepherds, the wise men, and His parents, they knew Jesus was different.

Hope had come.

Prayer: God, I want my hope to be in You only. Help me not be distracted by things that look good on the outside. My hope rests in Your love and goodness and in Your promises to me. In Your name I pray, Amen.

Activity: Make a Christmas list, but not for material items. What are you hoping for in your life? What intangible things can you ask for that only come from a Savior who came to give us hope?

DECEMBER 17

"I have told you this so that my joy may be in you and that your joy may be complete." John 15:11 (NIV)

Joy.

Joy to the world the Lord has come. We sing this song and hear it played multiple times during the season.

Oh, what joy! The long-awaited Messiah has come. And He's still here and available to us today.

It's said that happiness is a feeling based on your circumstances, but joy is an attitude. Joy is something we must *choose.*

It's because of Jesus that we *can* choose joy.

We can choose joy even when our circumstances don't seem so wonderful.

Going back to the verse: *"I have told you this."*

What did He tell us? He told us that He loves us with the Father's love.

Knowing and accepting God's love for us makes it possible for us to experience joy no matter the circumstances.

Prayer: Dear Jesus, thank You for joy that comes only from You. Help me not to base my feelings on circumstances but help me to have an attitude of joy no matter what is going on around me. Help my life to shine that light and share that joy with others. In Your Name, Amen.

Activity: Today choose not to allow your circumstances to dictate your feelings but instead choose joy, no matter what is going on around you.

DECEMBER 18

"Let the peace of Christ rule in your hearts, since as members of one body you were called to peace. And be thankful."
Colossians 3:15 (NIV)

The peace of Jesus Christ.

That's a peace that is different from any other. In fact, it is the only *true* peace.

How can we have peace in Christ? We put our hope in Him.

We can have peace, because we choose to be thankful no matter the circumstances around us.

Christ came so that we could have peace. Peace in our hearts and peace in our lives.

Peace floods us when we accept the sacrifice He made for us by coming to earth then dying on the cross for our sins.

During this holiday season, do you have that peace? The peace that comes only from knowing Him and putting your trust completely in Him as Lord and Savior of your life?

"Peace on earth. Good will to men." It can be more than a saying we hear this time of year.

The peace of Christ can be yours every single day.

Prayer: Dear Jesus, You came to bring peace. I need Your peace in my life today. Even when everything around me gets crazy, *especially* when it gets crazy, help my heart to be centered on You. I'm asking this in Your name, Amen.

Activity: Peace is about His presence. Although peace can happen in the midst of utter chaos, take some time today to get quiet. No matter what is going on around you, take a few moments and soak in His presence and allow His peace to settle over you.

DECEMBER 19

"Blessed is she who has believed that the Lord would fulfill his promises to her!" Luke 1:45 (NIV)

Oh, to believe and have faith like Mary!

Imagine with me for just a moment that you're a young teen girl, you've been visited by an angel and told that you are going to be the mother of the Son of God.

Who could or even would believe such a thing?! And if you believed it, would you be willing to do it?

This is a thought well beyond my wildest comprehension.

But Mary not only believed and was willing, she also embraced this special calling.

Do you find it hard to believe God's Word?

What about all the wonderful things He says about you?

That you are His child (*see John 1:12*).

That you are loved (*see Romans 8:38-39*).

That you are a temple of His Holy Spirit (*see 1 Corinthians 6:19-20*).

That He will provide (*see Philippians 4:19*).

His word is true. He fulfills His promises. You can count on it, my friend.

Prayer: Dear God, please help me be like Mary and believe Your word and have faith that Your promises to me will be fulfilled. Thank You for loving me and for being a faithful God. In Your Name I pray, Amen.

Activity: Search God's word and His promises. Find one that you will choose to believe for your life. Write it on a note card. Place your promise where you will see it everyday. He will fulfill His promises.

DECEMBER 20

"For with God nothing shall be impossible." Luke 1:37 (NIV)

You may have heard this verse before and may have even claimed it for something for which you were believing God.

For the longest time I had not put this verse with the message from the angel to Mary. I merely read this verse alone.

And yet, this is referring to one of the greatest miracles ever...that a virgin would become pregnant with the Son of God.

If indeed God has the power to do that, then absolutely nothing is impossible for our great God.

What is going on in your life right now? During this most wonderful time of year, is there something huge and seemingly impossible that you're facing or believing God for?

Dear friend, be encouraged. We serve a mighty and powerful God. *There is nothing impossible* with Him. In this season of miracles, when the unbelieving believe, He can do anything.

Are you giving Him room to be God? To be the great and all-powerful God that He is?

I hope so. I tend to limit Him or question Him at times. Do you find yourself doing the same?

Let's give Him room to be great in our lives and be the answer to our prayers in whatever way He chooses.

Prayer: Dear God, thank You for Your power and Your majesty. Thank You for the promise that nothing is impossible. Help me to trust and believe. I give You this thing now, and I believe that You will do it. In Jesus' name, Amen.

Activity: Donate food or clothes to a local pantry or shelter today. You may be the miracle someone else is waiting on. Let God use you today.

DECEMBER 21

"For unto us a child is born, unto us a son is given: and the government shall be upon his shoulder: and his name shall be called Wonderful, Counsellor, The mighty God, The everlasting Father, The Prince of Peace. Of the increase of his government and peace there shall be no end, upon the throne of David, and upon his kingdom, to order it, and to establish it with judgment and with justice from henceforth even for ever. The zeal of the Lord of hosts will perform this." Isaiah 9:6-7 (KJV)

This passage right here. These words. The prophecy of the coming Messiah. So much to take away from this portion of scripture.

Let's look at His names.

He is Counselor.

He is Mighty God.

He is Everlasting Father.

He is Prince of Peace.

This baby was and is everything that we need.

A child that carries the government on His shoulders. He would bear the weight of the world...for you and for me.

Who do you need Him to be to you today?

Do you need a counselor to comfort you and help you work through a problem or an issue? He is there for you with support and answers.

Do you need someone to show up in your life in a big way? He is Mighty!

Do you need to feel the love of a father? He is your Everlasting Father. He is waiting with open arms. Run into them.

Do you need peace? He is the Prince of Peace. In Him is peace and calm and quiet. Even when the world around you feels chaotic. Even as we draw near to Christmas Day and try to fit in yet another celebration. You will find peace in His presence.

What is weighing heavily on you in this moment? He bore the weight of the world. He can handle whatever it is that you bring to Him today.

Prayer: Dear God, here I am. I need You to be _____ to me.
Thank You for loving me enough to come and bear my burdens. I lay
them at Your feet. Amen.

Activity: Reach out to someone in need today. When we offer help
out of our own needs, we experience God in our world.

DECEMBER 22

"Glory to God in the highest, and on earth peace, good will toward men." Luke 2:14 (KJV)

Christmas Day is almost here! This holiday is a favorite for many.

Praises to God. Peace on earth. Goodwill to all.

But I realize it's not always that way, and it might not be *your* favorite time.

This may be a difficult time for you. Some years the Christmas season is better than others, because circumstances and situations arise.

Life happens. It's not always peace and joy and goodwill.

We face hard times and struggles. The difficulties may come in the form of a job situation or lack of finances. Sickness and injuries happen. Relationships ebb and flow.

This is life.

But I know that life in Christ is the only way to live. He came to bring us peace and to bring goodness to the world. It's because of His promises that we can say "Glory to God in the highest" even when things aren't so wonderful.

Are you struggling today to sing praise? Is it a struggle to read this verse and feel peace and happiness?

Friend, in Him are all good things. He came to Earth in a dirty stable. It wasn't glorious. Mary felt pain as she delivered the Son of God into the world. And yet, it was a time to praise Him.

With Him came all that we will ever need. In faith, will you say, "Glory to God in the highest, and on Earth peace, goodwill toward men"?

Prayer: Jesus, thank You for being everything that I need. Thank You for coming in the dark and dirty stable and giving me reason to say "Glory to God" even when things around me are not so glorious. Help me to rely on You. In Your precious name, Amen.

Activity: Play Christmas music today. Let the spirit of the season infiltrate your heart and your soul. Give Him glory today.

DECEMBER 23

"But Mary kept all these things, and pondered them in her heart." Luke 2:19 (KJV)

Moms, can you put yourself in Mary's place for a few minutes?

She was the chosen one to give birth to the Son of God. Such a calling I cannot even imagine.

But at the end of the day, she was a young girl and a new mother.

She had the same feelings that you and I did the first time we held our newborn baby. She marveled at all of His firsts...the first time He rolled over, His first words, His first steps.

I remember having the privilege to pray with Ethan when he was a little guy to accept Jesus into his heart. And I remember the day I got to baptize him. As I write this, I think of this past Mother's Day when he told me that he's considering seminary and possibly a path to priesthood.

On all those occasions, I thought back again to this verse and to Mary. I, like her, keep those special moments in my heart. They are times and experiences that I hold dear and am grateful for.

Whether you are a mom or a dad or an aunt, a sister, or a brother, or a friend, I know there is a person, or even people, in your life on whom you have had an influence. I'm sure there are special moments to ponder.

Prayer: Dear God, thank You for the special moments. Thank You for the example of Mary who had such a high calling and yet she shows that she is just like us...holding onto and cherishing special moments in her Child's life. In Your name, Amen.

Activity: Fix a warm drink, sit by a fire or in a cozy place, and ponder the special moments that you have been part of...for your children or another significant person in your life. What a privilege we have to be a part of God's plan!

DECEMBER 24

"And Mary said: "My soul magnifies the Lord, And my spirit has rejoiced in God my Savior." Luke 1:46-47 (NKJV)

What a joyous time of the year!

Everything seems a little better at Christmastime.

The lights seem brighter. The smells are more appealing. The sounds of the season are soothing. People slow down a bit and practice kindness more often.

This month it's easier to celebrate and be grateful.

Why is it that we wait until this time of year to rejoice?

There are moments each and every day that can be celebrated. Our Lord reigns. He came and now lives in us. We can rejoice daily for our salvation. We have a Savior who loves us.

Instead of thinking that Christmas is almost here and that it'll be over in a day or two, perhaps we can look at this as the beginning of a joyful coming year.

Prayer: Dear God, help me not to lose this spirit of thanksgiving and rejoicing that seems to come only at this time of year. I rejoice in You today and for all the days to come. I praise Your name. I love You, Jesus. Amen.

Activity: Turn up the Christmas music today. Sing and dance and celebrate our Savior.

DECEMBER 25

Merry Christmas!

It is here. That special day that we have been building up to.

Maybe you're reading this before everyone wakes up and the chaos ensues.

Perhaps you're reading this at the end of a long day of celebrations, and you're quite exhausted.

It could be that it's not even Christmas Day, but you've opened to this page anyway.

I'm not sure what your situation is at this moment, but I do know this: God loves you.

"For God so loved the world that he gave his one and only Son, that whoever believes in him shall not perish but have eternal life." John 3:16 (NIV)

He is the gift of Christmas.

New life is His gift to you and me. We can open that gift any day of the year. I pray that you have opened it and will allow Him to come and be part of your Christmas celebration.

May you know His gift of love in your life from this day forward.

Merry Christmas, Dear One.

DECEMBER 26

The Day After Letdown

The day after Christmas. It always comes.

All the hype and excitement is over. We hit the climax. Now what?

There may still be gifts under the tree or boxes and wrapping paper strewn across the floor. You may even have a gathering or two yet to attend, but for all intents and purposes, Christmas is over. One year until we do this all again.

I remember as a child feeling a huge letdown the day after Christmas. There had been so much energy and excitement building up to the big day and then it's over.

Just over.

The tree we had put up the day after Thanksgiving was already coming down. The lights weren't left on anymore.

But the truth is **this same Jesus that we celebrated yesterday still lives today.**

How can we keep that feeling alive in our hearts and our homes?

One thing I like to do is have a small nativity scene displayed in my house all year long.

We can keep the spirit of giving alive by looking for ways to bless others with our time, talents, or treasures.

Daily time in God's Word will keep us connected to our Savior.

Consider leaving the tree up an extra day. Keep the outside lights on. Read the Christmas story another time. Have a cup of hot chocolate by the fire.

The reason for the season is still alive and well, and we can celebrate Him 365 days of the year.

DECEMBER 27

Gratitude

Do you have a daily gratitude practice?

The Bible says, "*A merry heart does good like a medicine*" (see Proverbs 17:22).

One of the quickest ways to change our attitude is to count our blessings.

"Enter his gates with thanksgiving and his courts with praise; give thanks to him and praise his name." Psalm 100:4 (NIV)

We may not always feel festive, but we can make a choice to set our minds towards gratitude.

I find the best way to do this is to make it a daily practice.

I spend time each evening writing down three things from the day for which I'm grateful. It may be something simple like the smell of coffee or an evening at home. It might be a job promotion or the birth of a new baby.

Some days the list will come quickly and easily. Other days it may take some time to get your heart and mind in a place of thanksgiving.

Once you start the daily practice, you'll become more aware of blessings throughout the day and begin making mental notes to write those things down later in the evening.

Whether you choose to begin your day with gratitude or end your day that way, consider making a gratitude list part of your daily habit. Write it down so you can glance back and be encouraged by God's goodness. I guarantee that it will come in handy from time to time.

"Every good and perfect gift is from above, coming down from the Father of the heavenly lights, who does not change like shifting shadows." James 1:17 (NIV)

Start your list today. Take the space below and list out some things for which you are grateful. There's nothing too big or too small. Expect God to show up each and every day. I know He will.

DECEMBER 28

Taking Inventory

It's time to take inventory. Let's look at it like a brain dump.

Growth comes from acknowledging both the wins and losses and noting the highs and lows.

This short time between Christmas and the new year tends to be a time for reflection. Things calm down for a few days. Let's take advantage of this lull and take a look back on our year and glance forward to what we want for the year ahead.

Too often we skim over our wins, minimizing them or taking them for granted. It's important to acknowledge when we reach a goal or take a step in the right direction. It's those steps on which we build and continue moving forward.

What were some things that went well over the last year? What progress, however small it may seem, did you make...in your health, finances, relationships, etc.? Think about all areas of your life.

Think back to times when you felt like things were going well. What was happening at that time? How were you spending your days? Who were you with?

Now think about areas where you felt like you struggled? When was this going on? Who, if anyone, was involved?

Perhaps you have two sheets of paper or divide your paper in half. On one sheet or one side, list the positives, the wins, and the highlights. On the other sheet or half of the paper, list the struggles and areas that you feel you need to improve upon.

Once you have your lists, sit with them awhile. Focus on the wins and the progress you have made. What can you continue doing or build on for the coming year? Next, consider what you learned during the struggles. What will you do differently going forward?

This is a good time to let go of things that may be holding you back and grab onto hope for the future.

DECEMBER 29

How to pick a word and verse for the new year

Picking a word for the year is common these days. People choose a word or phrase that sets their intention and gives them focus for the year.

Recently I got intentional about this process. I spend time reading God's Word, reflecting, and praying to discern what He wants my focus to be for the year. Not only do I want a word, but I also tie it to scripture so that I have His truth to guide me throughout the year.

For instance, one year my word was *beneficial*. The verse that went along with it was I Corinthians 10:23 (NKJV), "All things are lawful for me, but not all things are helpful; all things are lawful for me, but not all things edify." Essentially, everything is permissible but not everything is beneficial.

Not only would this be in regards to what I put into my mouth but this would also have an impact on what came out of my mouth, my words and my actions. While I was not perfect (just ask my family!), I had a focus. I had an intention. I had something by which to measure my words, my actions, the foods I chose, my schedule, etc. Everything came back to this one word and whether or not it was beneficial for me, for my family, and for those around me.

Another year my word was *run*.

It didn't have anything to do with the physical activity I love to do. Yes, every year I have some fitness goals, but that year it was about Hebrews 12:1.

It was about *"laying aside the weight and sin,"* those things that were distracting me and holding me back. And then *"run with endurance the race set before us"* which told me to run *my* race. In essence, get focused and go in the direction God is leading.

If this is something that you feel will be helpful to you in the coming year, I encourage you to take some time today and go through this process.

1. Grab your Bible and a notebook and go somewhere to be alone.

2. Pray. Ask God to clear your mind and to help you listen.

3. Consider the inventory you took yesterday. How was the last year, and what are you anticipating for the coming year?

4. Jot down words and phrases that start coming to you.

5. Search for scripture that goes along with the words or search the particular word that the Holy Spirit is giving to you.

6. Pray over your list.

Some years I have had multiple words and verses, and it's taken me a few days or even a week or two to settle on what my focus needs to be. Other times the word and verse came quickly and easily, and I knew right away.

There is no right or wrong way to do this process. The key is to listen to the Holy Spirit's prompting and to be obedient.

"For the word of God is alive and active." Hebrews 4:12 (NIV)

DECEMBER 30

Set yourself up for the best year yet

Are you ready for your best year yet?

Over the last few days you've taken time to practice gratitude, take inventory, acknowledge your highs and lows, and to consider a word and verse for the year.

Now it's time to focus, commit, and put your plans into action.

How exactly do we set ourselves up for our best year yet?

First, focus inward.

Our plans can't be based on what someone else is doing or a success someone else had with a certain thing or following a particular program.

We are all unique! It's the wonderful way that God made us to be different. And thus we have to learn our own bodies...how we respond to various foods and exercise...and honor our own lives...our likes and dislikes, our schedules and abilities.

Some questions to ask yourself when you start making goals and setting intentions for the year are these:

- WHY do I want this thing? This question is so important!

  - If your motivation comes from a place of guilt or shame or punishing yourself, it won't last. The follow through won't come.

- Will this make me a better person? Will this improve my interactions with my friends, family, loved ones?

- Is there biblical truth that I can apply? Have you checked out scripture? Is there a scripture that can become your prayer, your foundation, or your guide to support this plan for the new year?

- Is this sustainable? Can you see yourself doing this thing or adapting to this change three months from now, six months, or even a year?

Next, commit.

Once we've done this work, we should be confident that we're headed in the right direction. This confidence will help us keep our eyes on our own paper and not get distracted by what someone else is doing.

When our friend is talking about the detox she is doing or the new exercise plan she is following, we won't second guess the direction we're headed. This will only delay our own progress.

Finally, implement the steps to make lasting change.

The key here is to understand that results don't happen overnight. We're working towards a lifestyle. Lasting change will come when you commit to the process. This will eventually become a seamless way to live.

The best part is next year you won't be stressing and obsessing over the changes that you need to make. You'll simply continue living and doing life the way you have established it.

DECEMBER 31

Cheers to the New Year

"Lord, according to your Word, if I wholeheartedly commit whatever I do to you, my plans will succeed. (see Proverbs 16:3) Lord, I acknowledge that the heart of committing any plan to You is seeking *Your* plan. Show me the right path, Father!" (from Beth Moore's *Praying God's Word*)

I pray this prayer often. And now at the beginning of a new year, it is the perfect time to pray this and give the year to the Lord.

More scriptures to reflect on as you embark on this new year...

"Because of the Lord's great love we are not consumed, for his compassions never fail. They are new every morning; great is your faithfulness. I say to myself, The Lord is my portion; therefore, I will wait for him." Lamentations 3:22-24 (NIV) **Today can be a new day!**

"For I know the plans I have for you," declares the Lord, *"plans to prosper you and not to harm you, plans to give you a hope and a future."* Jeremiah 29:11 (NIV) **His plans for you are good!**

"See, I am doing a new thing! Now it springs up; do you not perceive it? I am making a way in the wilderness and streams in the wasteland." Isaiah 43:19 (NIV) **Be ready for open doors and new opportunities!**

"He put a new song in my mouth, a hymn of praise to our God. Many will see and fear the Lord and put their trust in him." Psalm 40:3 (NIV) **Praise the Lord for what He is going to do in you and through you!**

"To be made new in the attitude of your minds; and to put on the new self, created to be like God in true righteousness and holiness." Ephesians 4:23-24 (NIV) **It's time for a new attitude!**

"Therefore, if anyone is in Christ, he is a new creation; old things have passed away, behold, all things have become new." 2 Corinthians 5:17 (NKJV) **If you've never said yes to Christ, now is the time.** He can make you new! Even if you have said yes but haven't given Him every part of you, if you're still holding onto an area of your life, give it to Him now.

May all things be new for you this year!

EPILOGUE

So the question is always this...What will I do with this Jesus?

He has come to this world. He is a gift for you and for me.

Will I rejoice over Him?

Will I regift Him, and so share Him with others?

Will I put Him aside and then forget about Him?

Will I focus on Him this one time of year but then go back to everything else that gets more of my attention?

Each and every year at this time we come face to face with this Jesus once again. Reminders of His coming into the world are all around us.

For some, this is not new. We try to live everyday with our eyes on Jesus celebrating Who He is and what He came to do for us. For others of us, we allow the cares of the world to distract us until we've wandered far away.

It doesn't have to be like this. This year can be different. We can have a renewed awe of this Jesus, *our* Jesus, and invite Him fully into our lives and allow Him to be all that He came to be for each and every one of us.

So again, what will you do with Jesus this year?

It is my prayer that He will be as real to you one month from now, and the month after that and the month after that and so on, as He is today.

Merry Christmas and Happy New Year!

ABOUT THE AUTHOR

Marsha Apsley is a counselor and is passionate about helping women live fit and free. She does this by focusing on whole person health and wellness with an emphasis on how women feel about themselves. She believes that a healthy lifestyle needs to be built on a firm foundation of faith.

She is the author of 40 Days of Faith and Fitness: A Devotional Journal and a 6 Week Guide to Building a Healthy Life on a Foundation of Faith.

Marsha is a wife and mom of two sons. She loves to run and bike and enjoy a cup of coffee with friends. She believes everyday is better when it includes a little chocolate.

For support and encouragement on your faith and fitness journey, please visit her website www.marshaapsley.com or find her on social media @marshaapsley. If you'd like to be part of a tribe of women who are building a healthy life on a foundation of faith, join Marsha's free Facebook group Faith and Fitness with Marsha. It's a sisterhood of women who have found that we are stronger together. The doors are always open. To contact Marsha to speak at your next event, email her at marsha@marshaapsley.com.

Made in the USA
Monee, IL
25 November 2022

18441299R00049